Y0-CFQ-098

Copyright © 1987 by Casterman. English language translation copyright © 1987 by Simon & Schuster, Inc. All rights reserved, including the right of reproduction in whole or in part in any form. Published by Little Simon, A Division of Simon & Schuster, Inc., 1230 Avenue of the Americas, New York, New York 10020. Originally published in France as La Nature by Casterman, 1987. Published pursuant to agreement with Casterman, Paris. LITTLE SIMON and colophon are trademarks of Simon & Schuster, Inc. Manufactured in Belgium.
10 9 8 7 6 5 4 3 2 1
Library of Congress Cataloging in Publication Data   ISBN: 0-671-66139-6

SHOW ME MY WORLD

OUT AND ABOUT

BY JEAN PIERRE-HORLIN
ILLUSTRATED BY FRANCINE DE BOECK

LITTLE SIMON
PUBLISHED BY SIMON & SCHUSTER INC., NEW YORK

On The Farm

Chickens peck.
Nicky is afraid of the chicken.
Rosie is not afraid.
Goats butt.
Nicky is afraid of the goat.
Rosie is not afraid.
Donkeys kick.
Nicky is afraid of the donkey.
Rosie is not afraid.
Cows switch their tails.
Nicky is afraid of the cow.
Rosie is not afraid.
Cats scratch.
Nicky is afraid of the cat.
Rosie is not afraid.
A mouse doesn't peck, or butt, or kick,
or switch its tail, or scratch.
Nicky is not afraid of the mouse…
but why is Rosie standing on a chair?

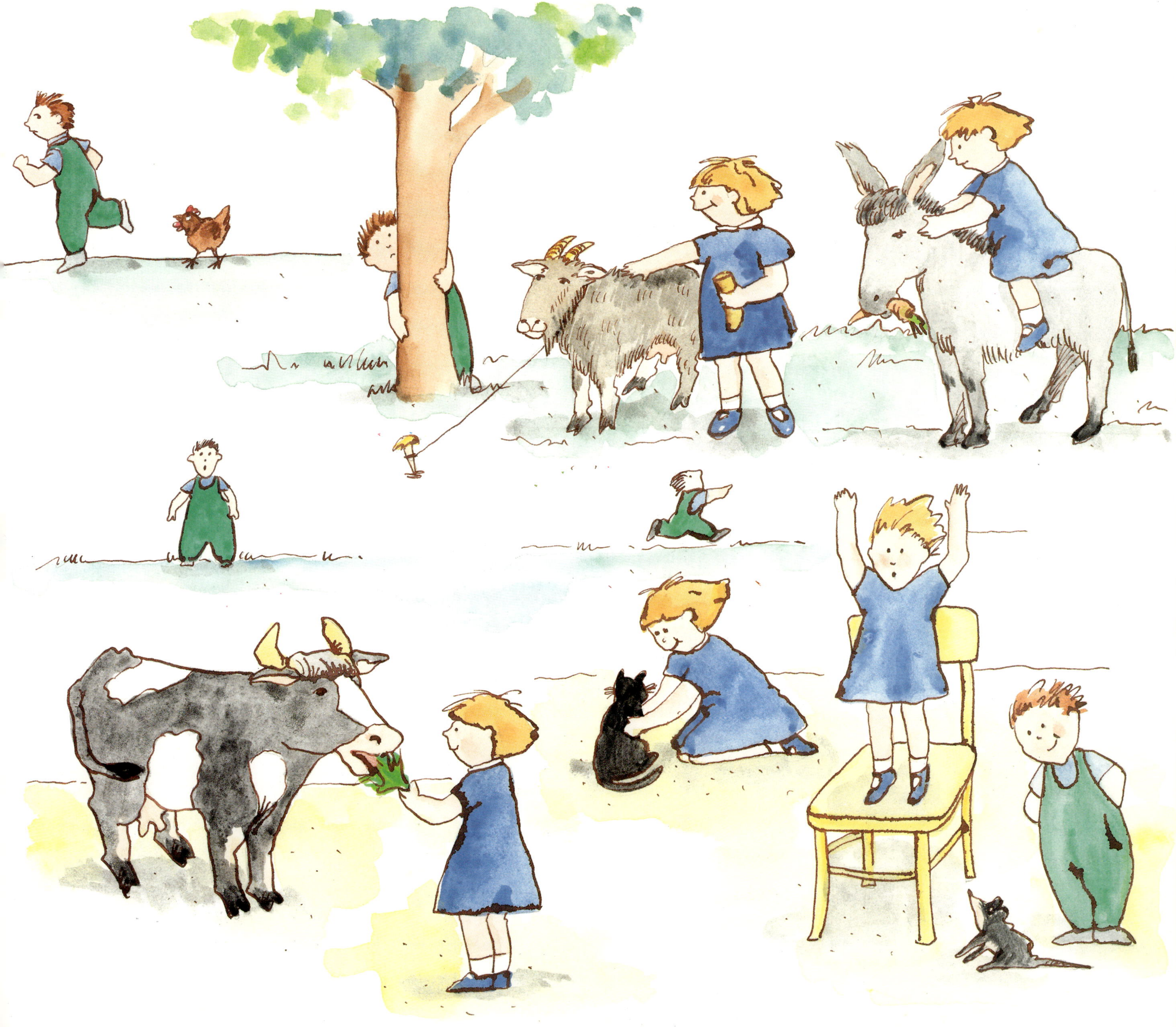

ROSIE'S TURTLE

Rosie wins a prize at a carnival booth.
It's a turtle. She puts it in an aquarium
with some rocks, and calls it Abigail.
But the next day, Abigail escapes.
Albigail is always escaping!
Rosie finds her in the windowbox,
and on the doormat.
One day when Abigail escapes,
Rosie cannot find her anywhere.
Is Abigail gone for good?
"Maybe the neighbor's cat ate her?"
sobs Rosie.
She opens her drawer to get a handkerchief
—there's Abigail!

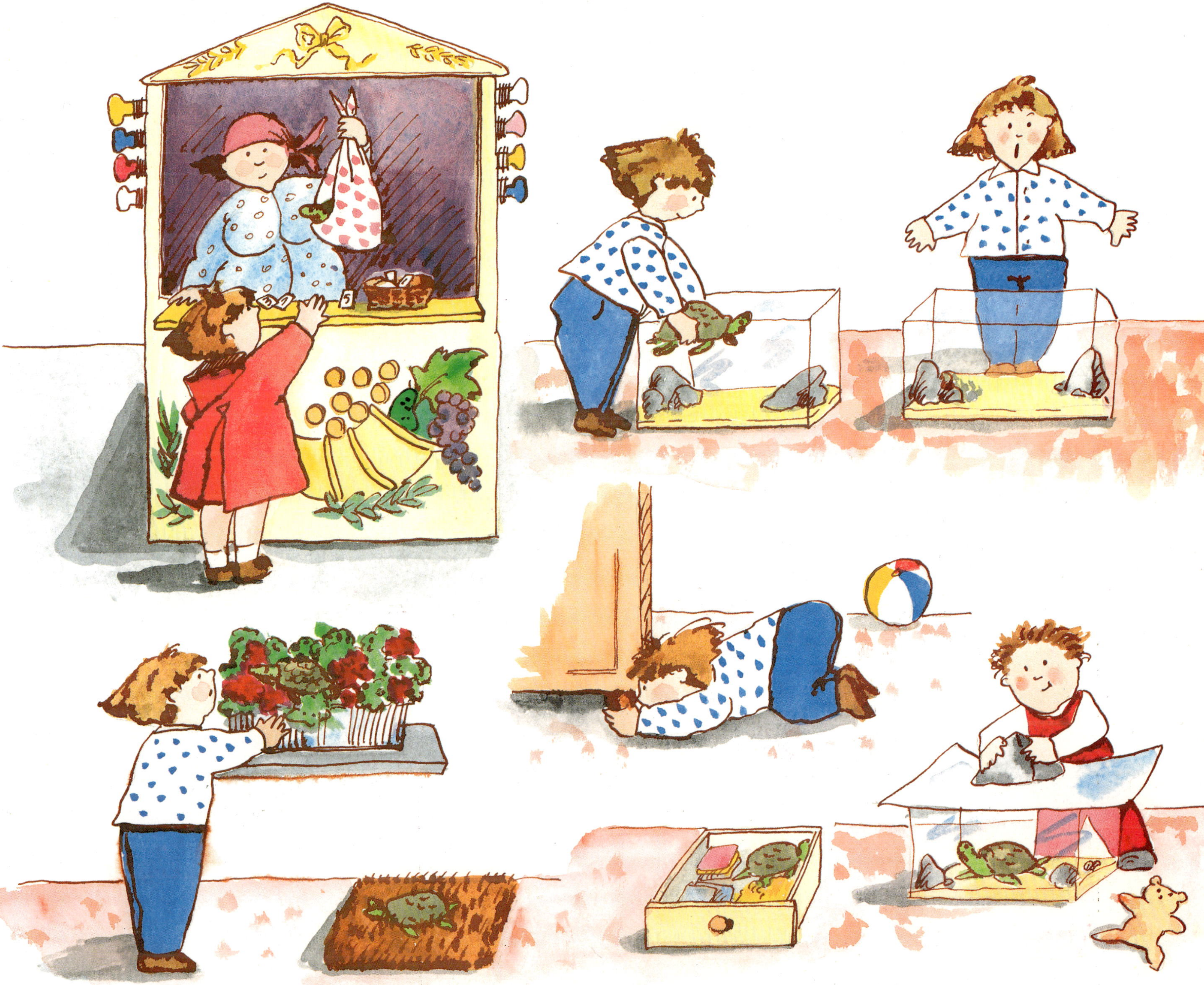

The Ducks

Father, Rosie, and baby Sam go to the park.
Rosie feeds the ducks.
The more bread Rosie throws,
the closer the ducks come.
They waddle right out of the water!
"Time to go home for dinner," says Father,
but the ducks are still hungry.
They follow Rosie—*quack! quack! quack!*—
out of the park,
right to her front door.
The ducks want dinner, too.

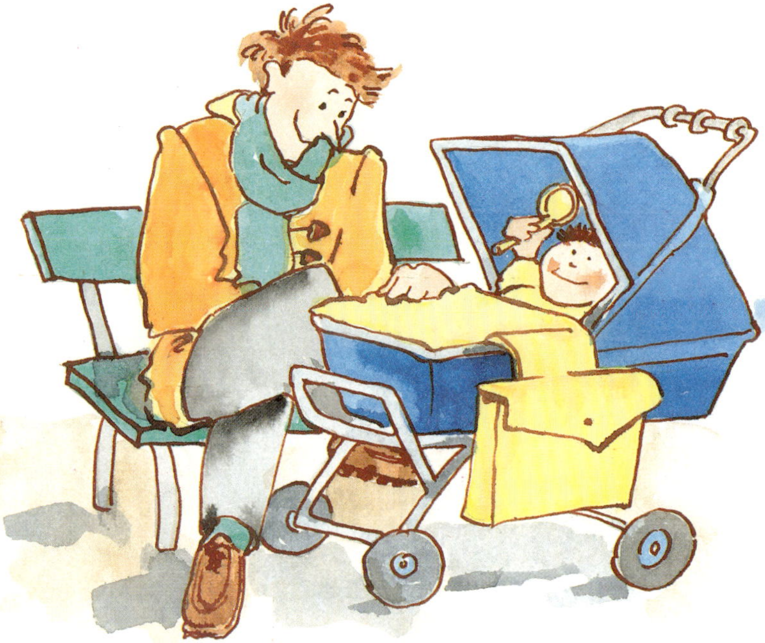

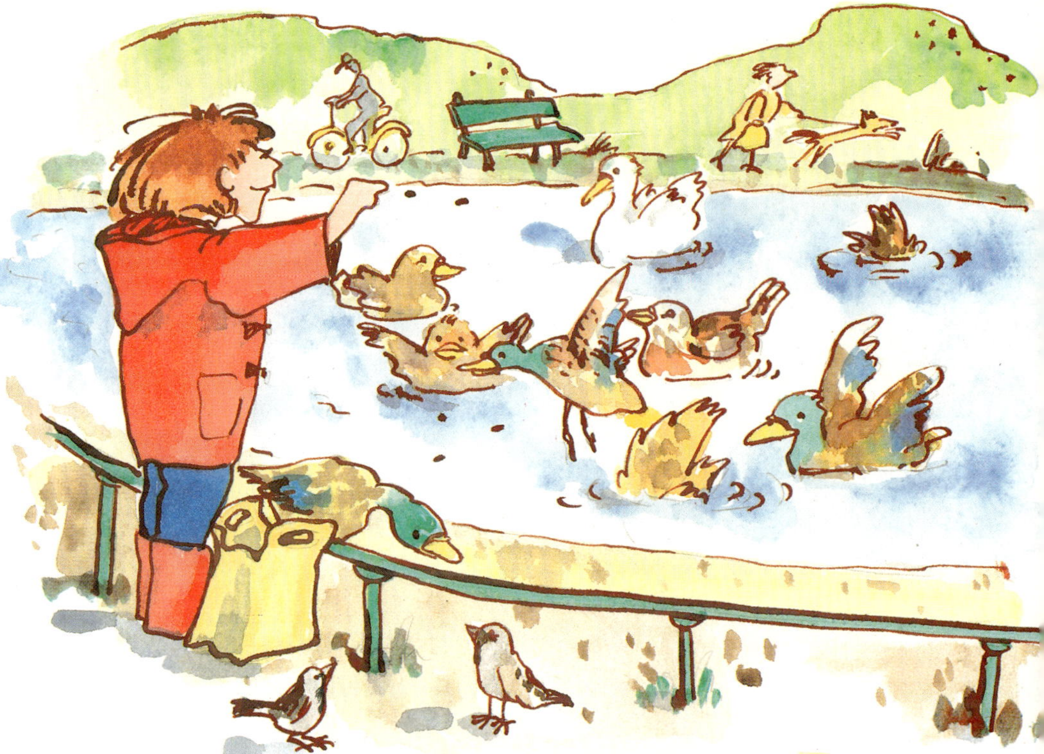

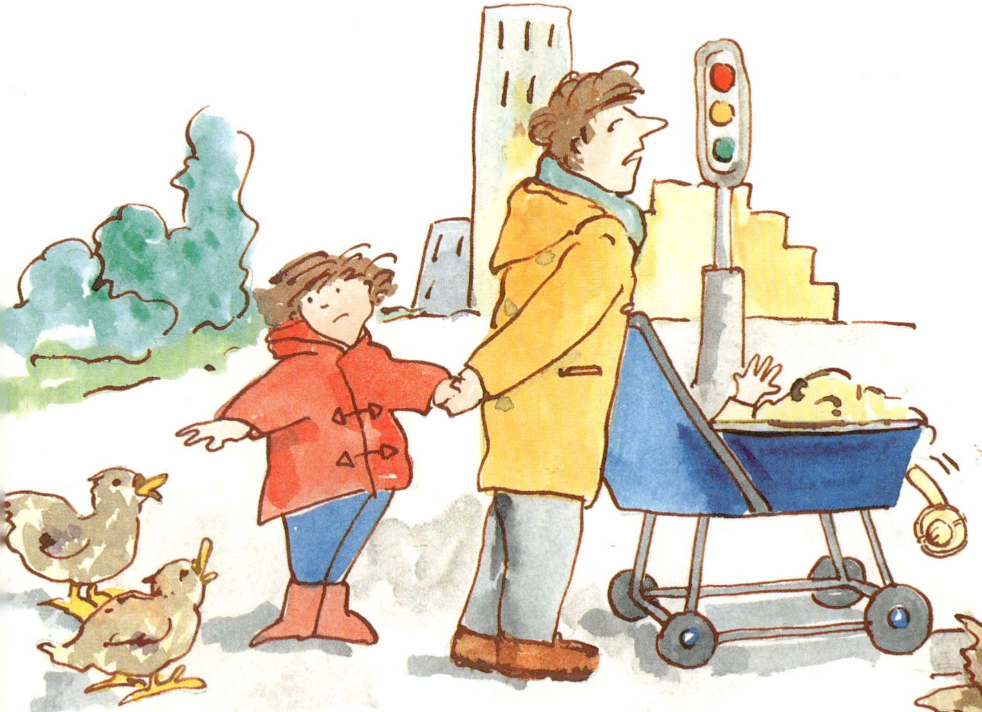

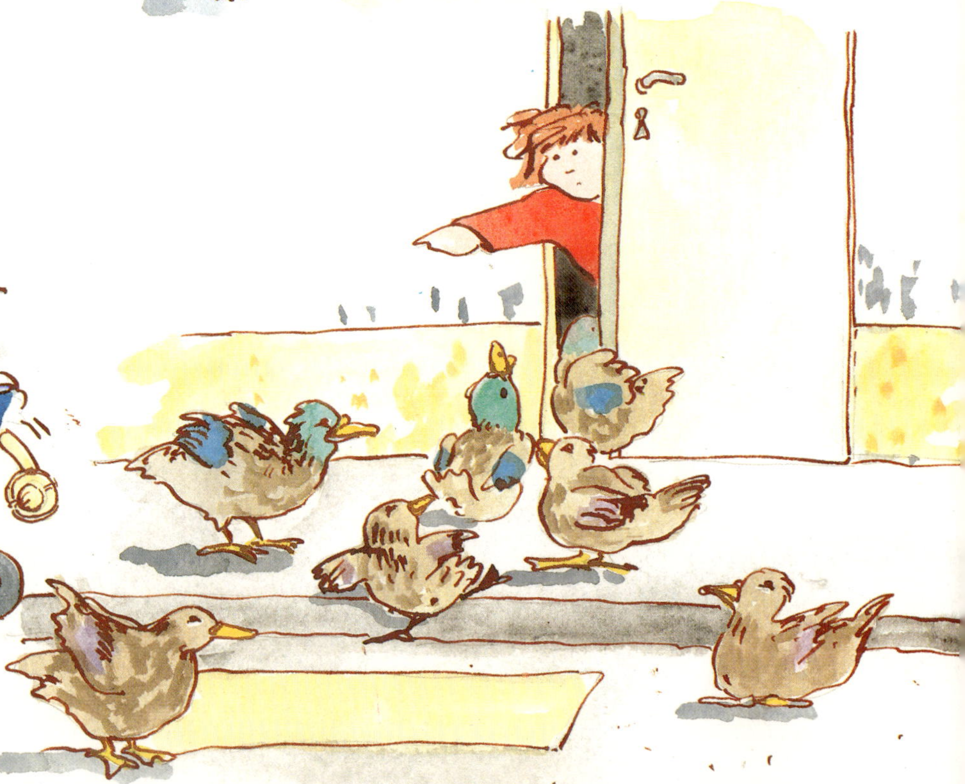

IN THE COUNTRY

Grandfather takes Rosie and Nicky
to the country.
Nicky catches some little fish in the stream.
Rosie puts snails in a cardboard box.
Nicky's fish can live in the bathtub.
But where are the snails? *Uh-oh*.
Rosie left the box in the car!

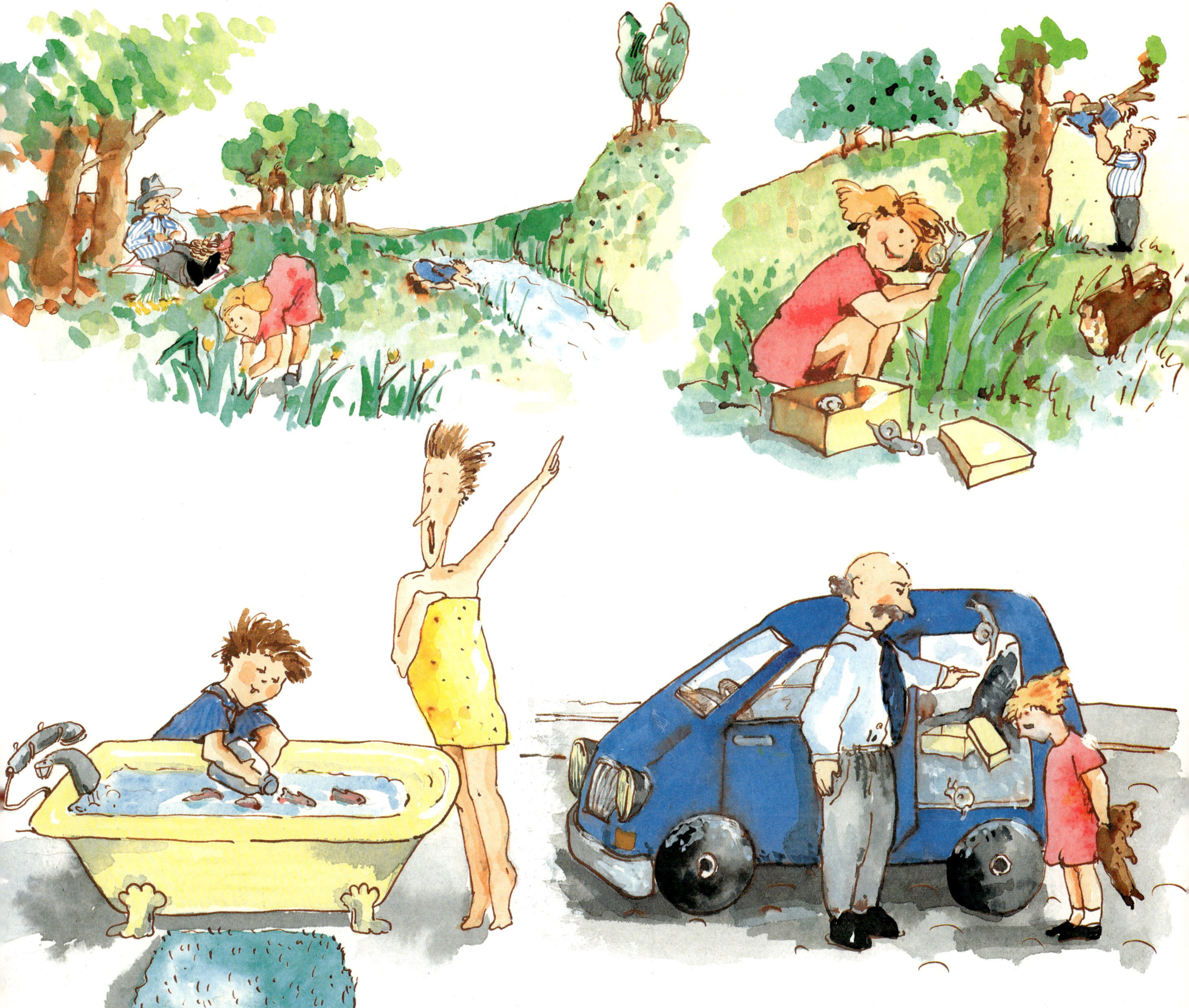

THE HAMSTER

Cousin Laura's hamsters have babies.
Laura gives one to Rosie and Nicky.
They call him Hector.
Hector is very happy in his new home.
But then, one day, Rosie finds Hector
lying on his back.
He is dead.
Nicky digs a hole in the garden.
Rosie puts some cotton in a box
and lays Hector on it.
She puts the box in the bottom of the hole.
Rosie cries. Nicky cries, too.
Mommy has tears in her eyes.
She puts flowers on Hector's grave.

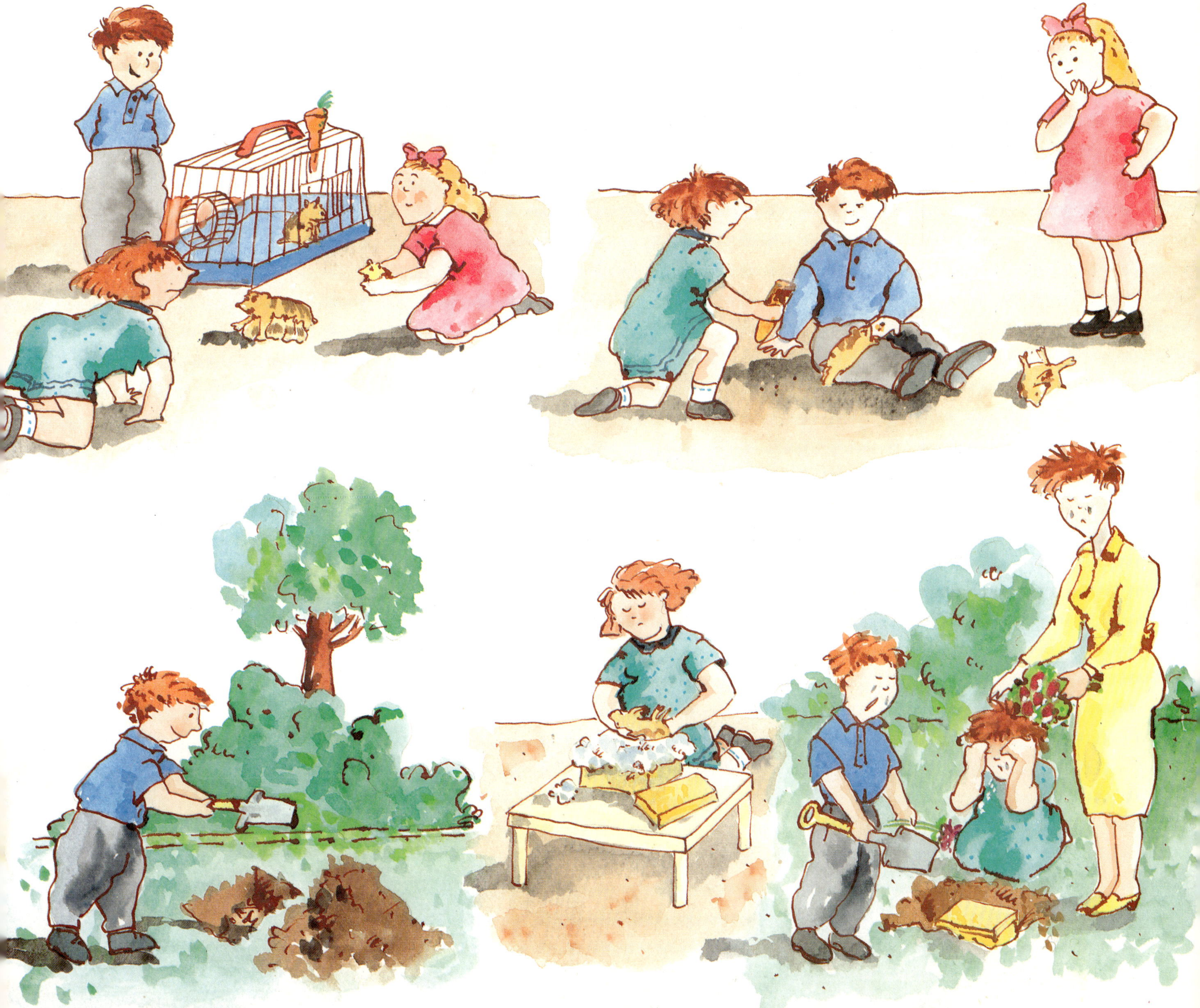

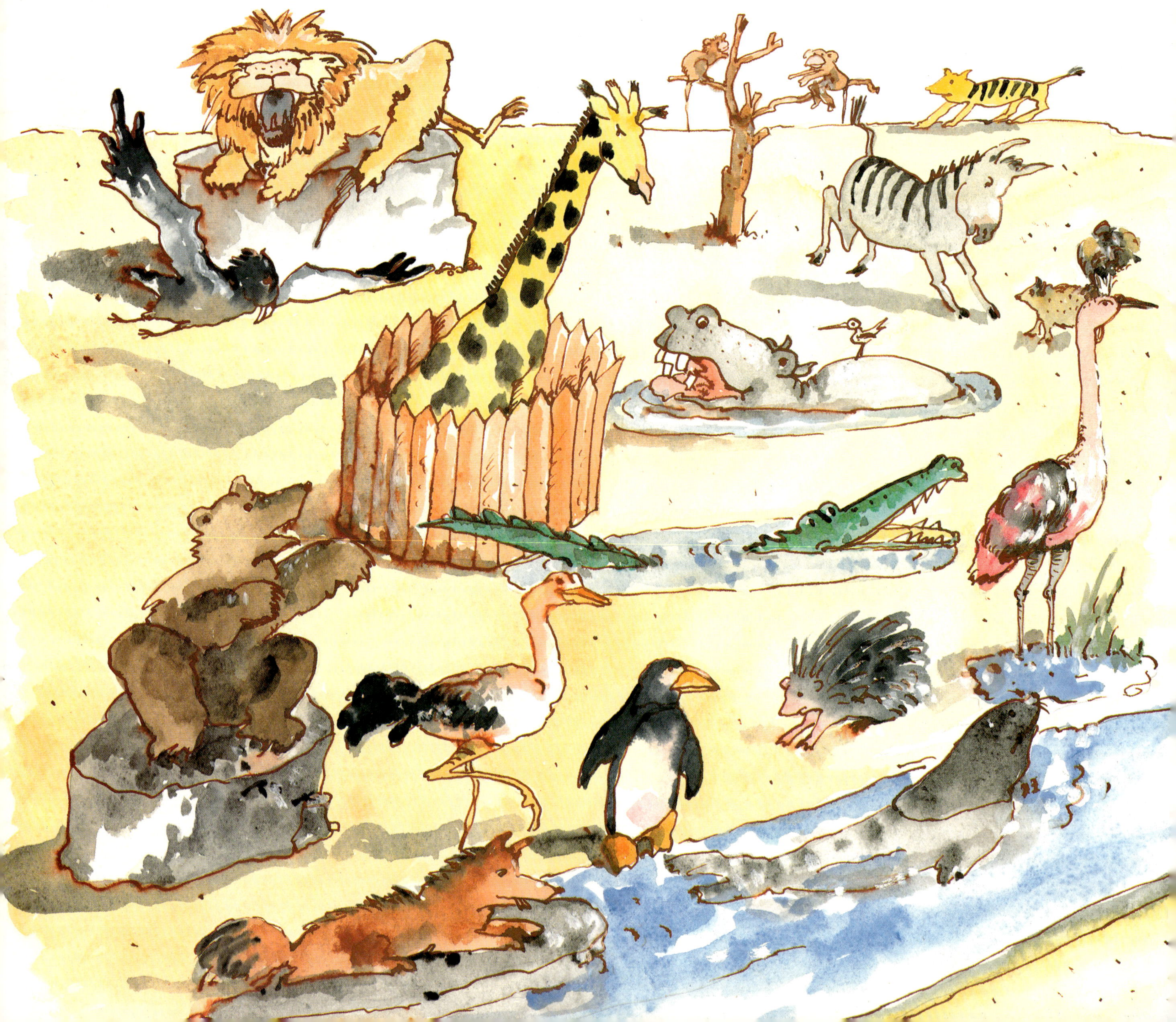

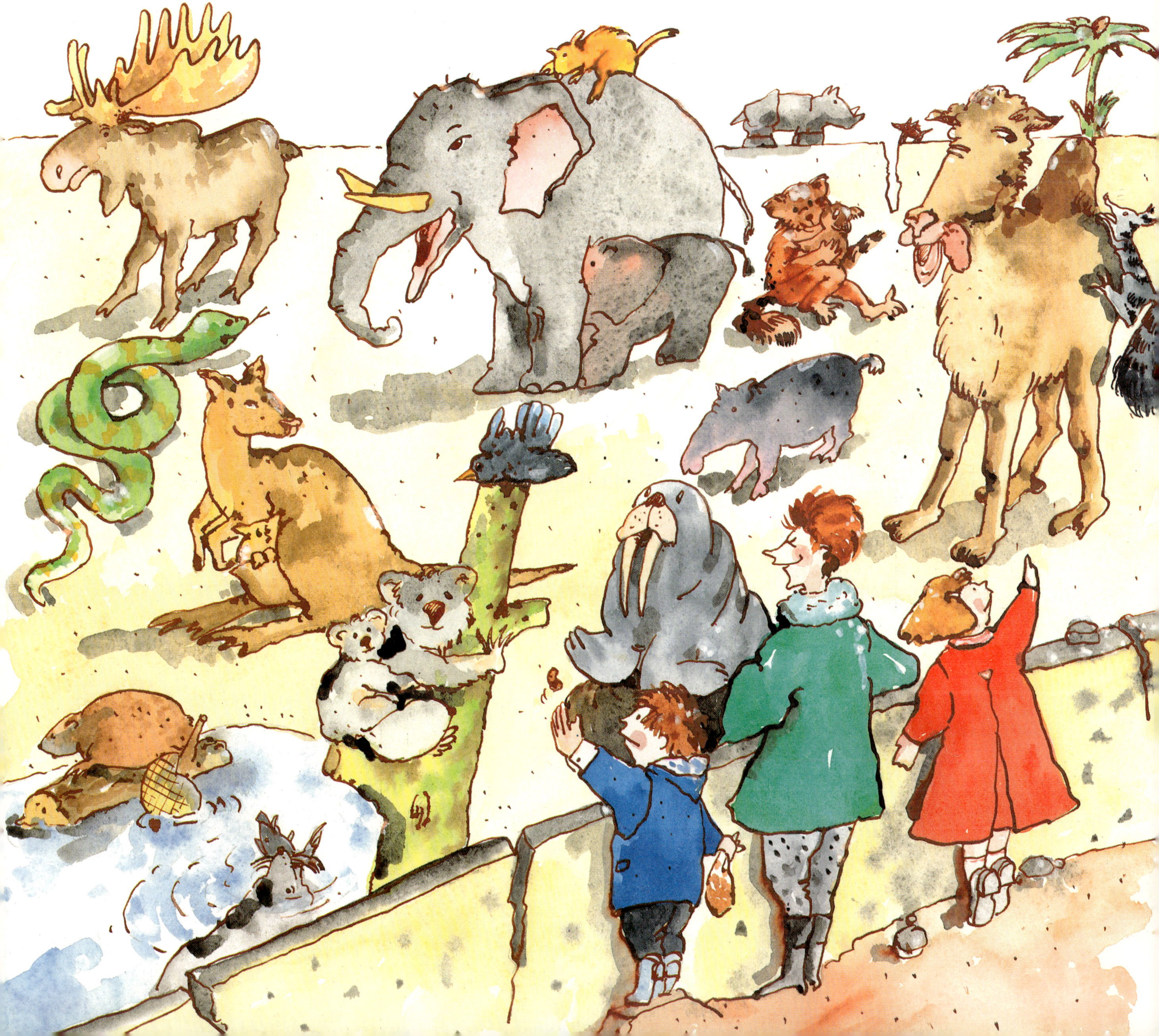

The Mice

Nicky and Rosie hear noises in the attic.
They go and take a look.
They crouch down and wait quietly—
and two tiny grey mice appear.
Rosie says, "Don't tell Daddy."
Every day, Nicky and Rosie
go up to the attic.
They leave a crust of bread
or a piece of cheese.
Now, the mice no longer run away
when they come.
But one day
there are no longer
two mice in the attic.
There are eight!

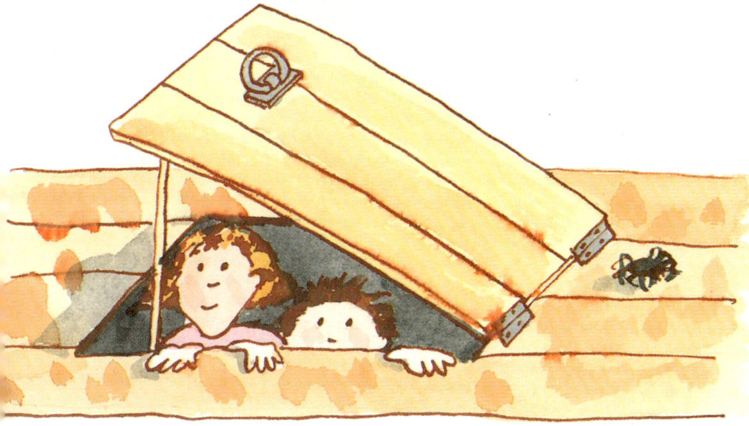

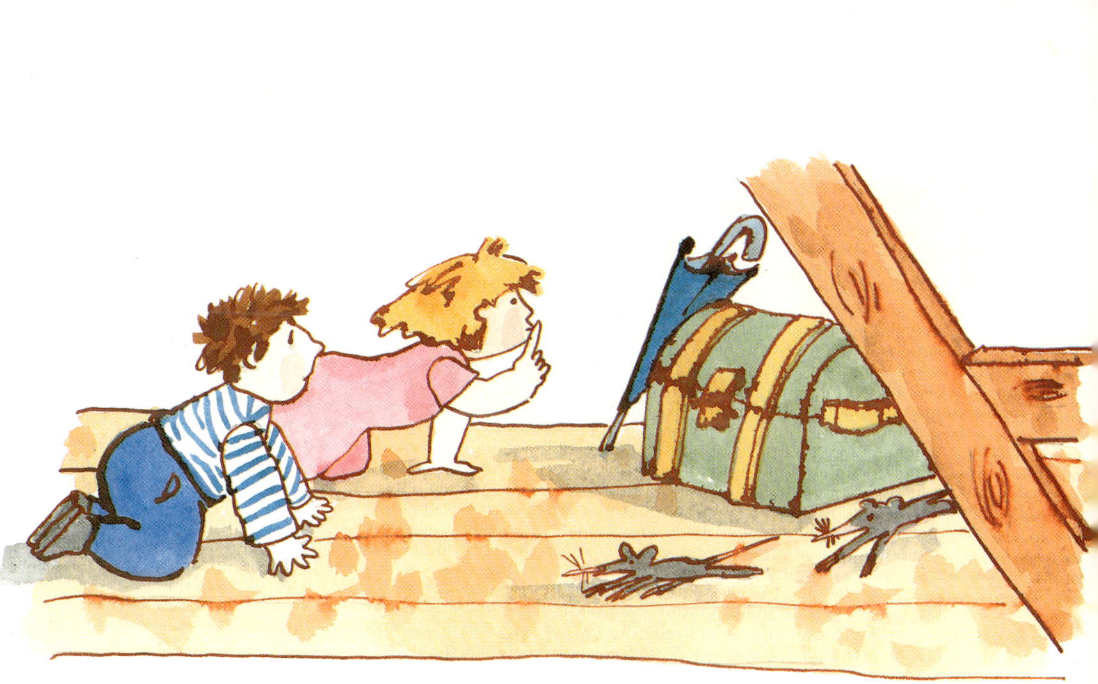

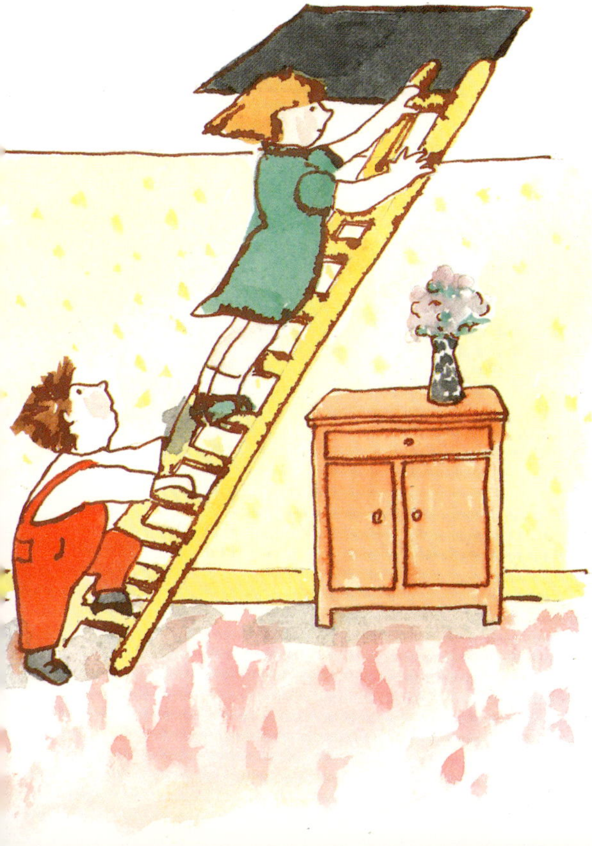

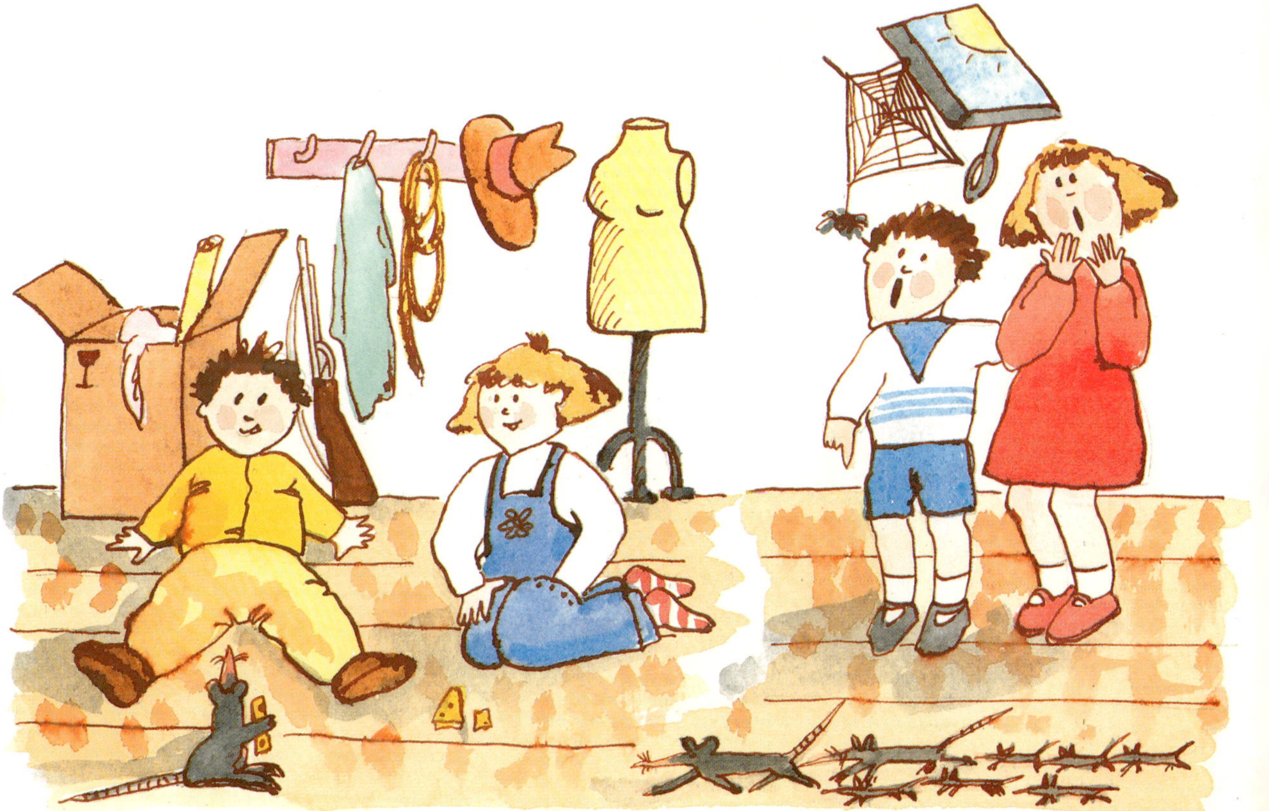

GRANDFATHER'S GARDEN

Grandfather is ready to plant his garden.
"What are in those packages?" asks Nicky. "Candy?"
"No," says Grandfather, "they're seeds.
Carrot seeds, radish seeds, celery seeds,
all kinds of seeds."
"Can we help?" begs Rosie.
"All right," says Grandfather,
"But let me have some coffee, first."
One by one, Nicky opens the packages
and pours the seeds into a box.
Rosie mixes well, just like when Mommy makes a cake.
"What are you doing?" calls Grandfather.
"We've gotten all the seeds ready,"
say Rosie and Nicky,
"Now all you have to do is put them in the ground."

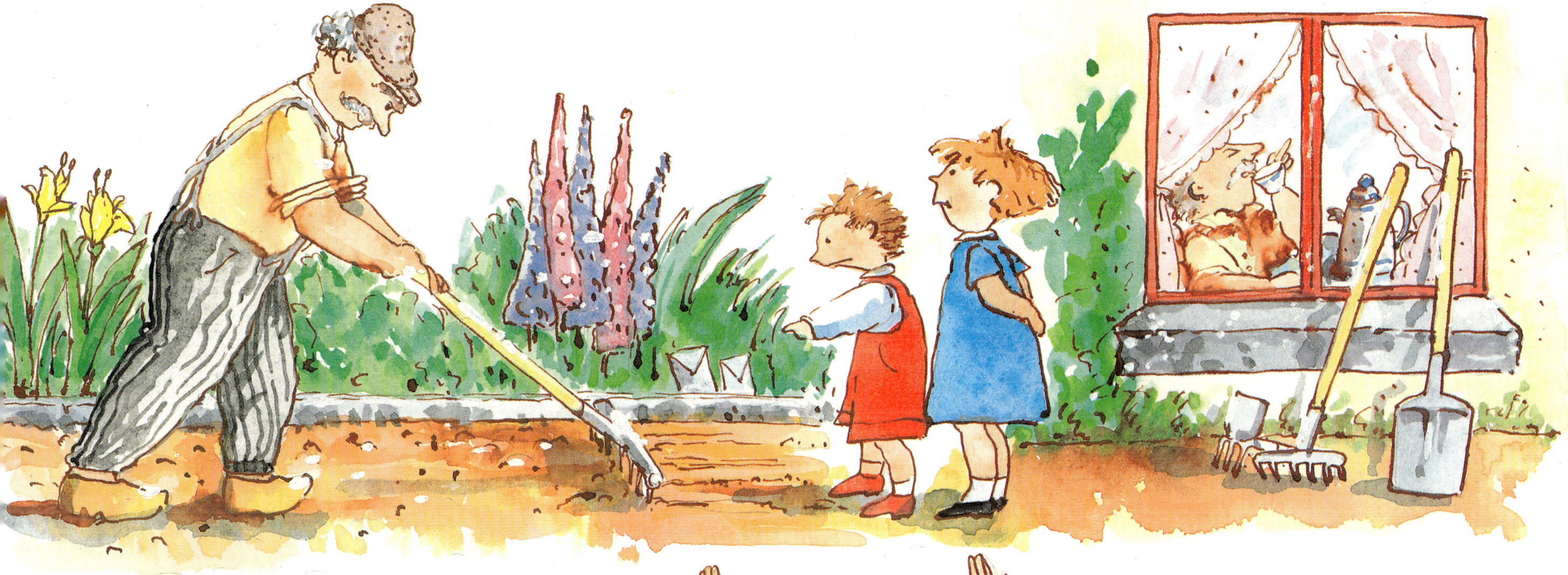
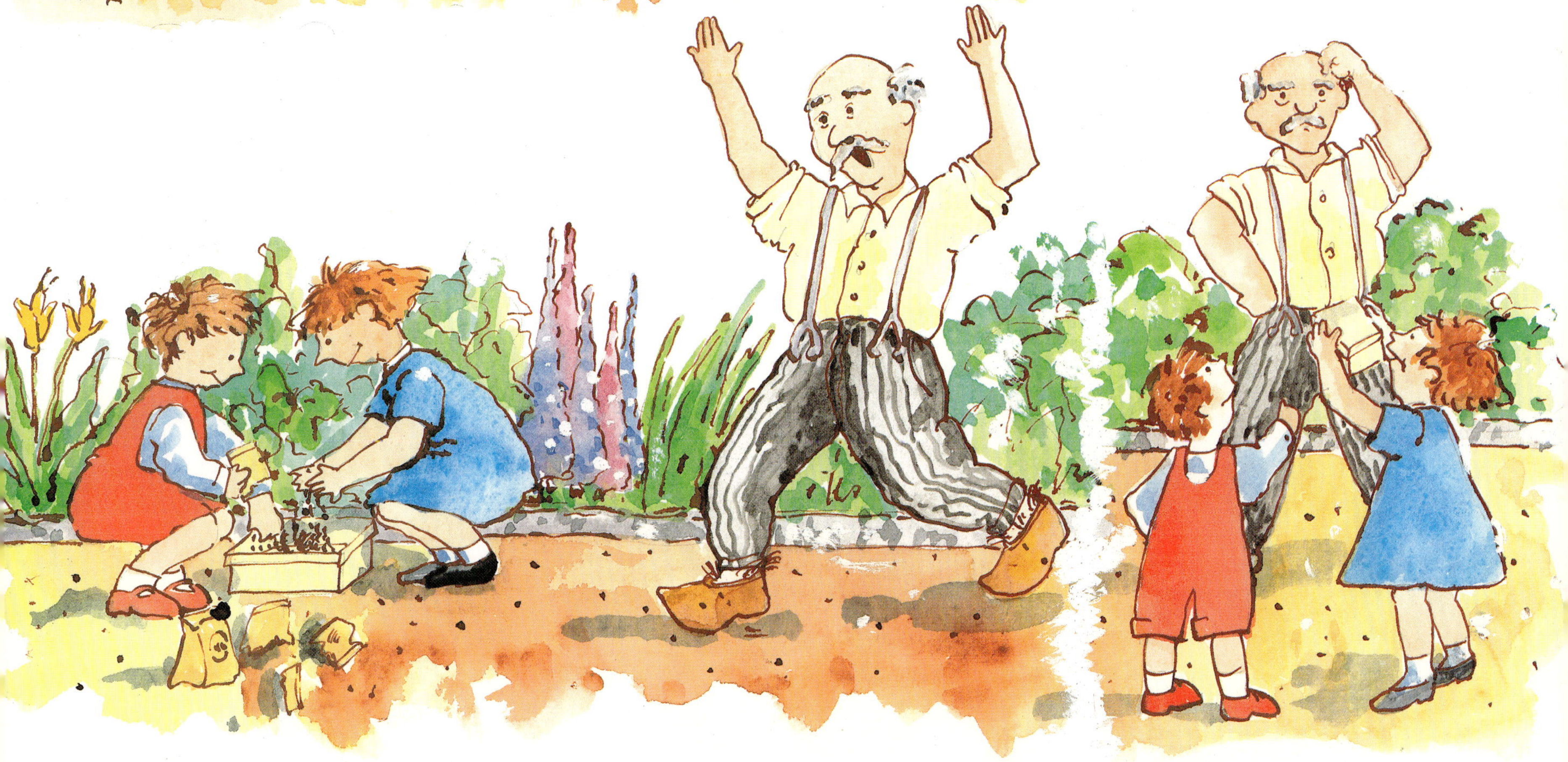

THE FROG

"Rosie, look!" says Nicky.
"A frog. Let's catch it!"
Plunk.
"Where is it, Nicky?"
Rosie turns around.
Behind her is a cow.
Plunk! Plunk!
Rosie and Nicky jump in the pond.
"Rosie! The frog! The frog!"
"Where is it, Nicky?"
"It's on your head!"

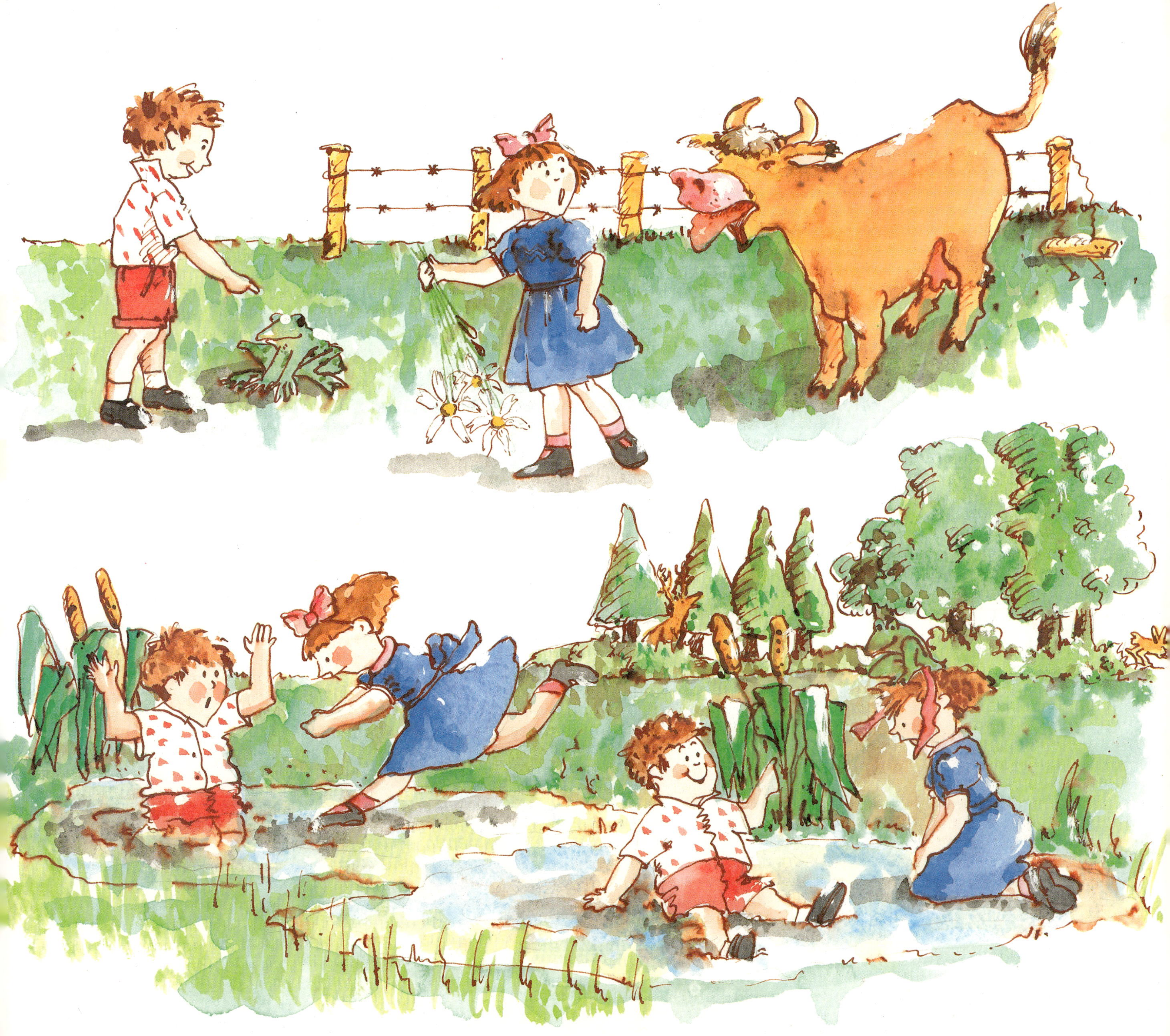

THE SEEDS

Rosie asks Father for a flower pot.
Nicky and Rosie fill the pot with dirt
and plant some seeds.
Rosie puts the pot in her bedroom.
Every day she waters it. Two small leaves appear...
then four, then eight.
The plant is growing.
Yellow flowers sprout
and then the flowers droop.
But the plant keeps growing.
And one day Rosie and Nicky find cucumbers
growing on the plant!

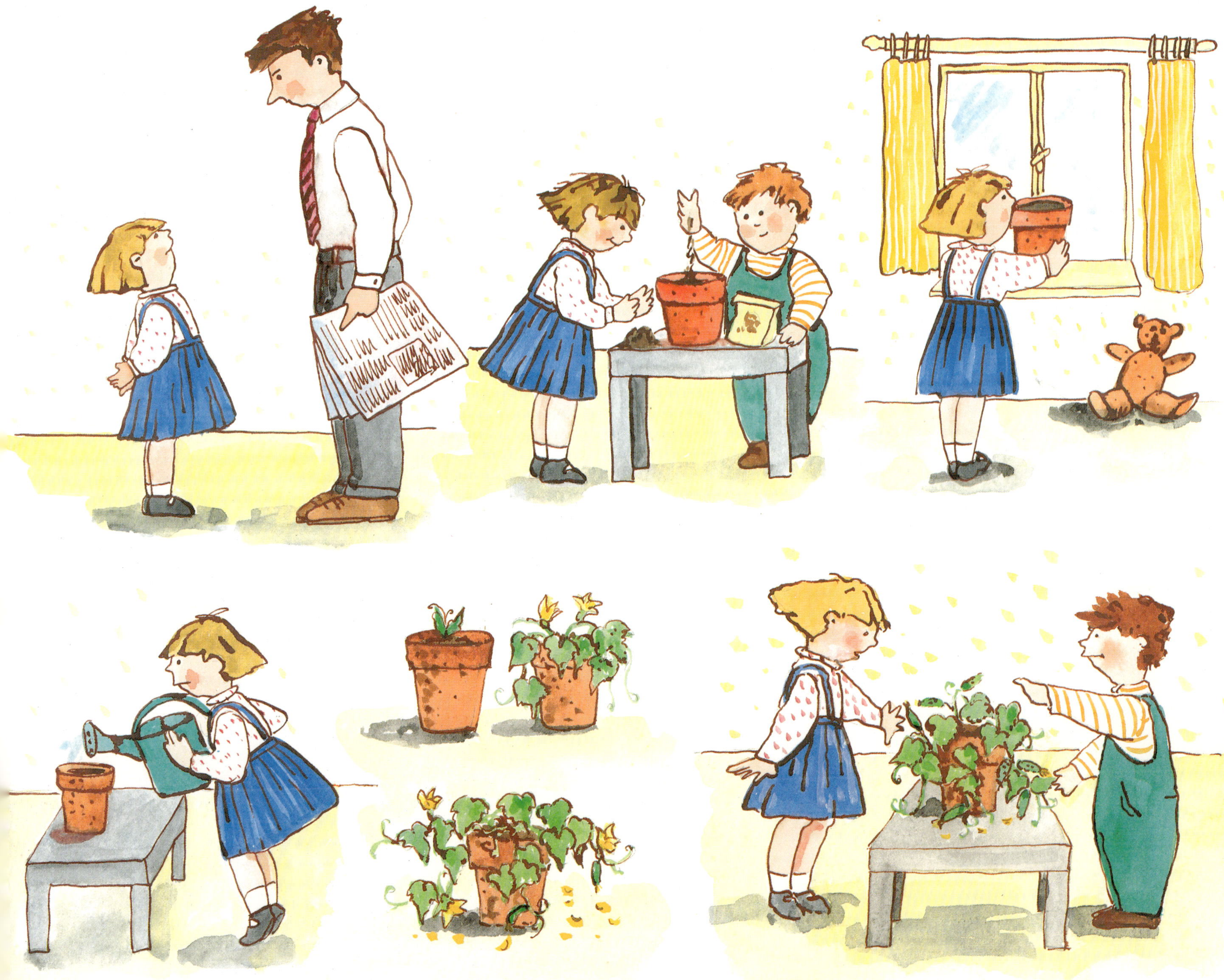

The Rabbits

Rosie and Nicky go to the farm with Father
to buy milk and butter.
Nicky wants to give a cracker to the rabbits.
He opens the door of the cage and—*oops*!
—the rabbits escape.
Rosie and Nicky run after the rabbits.
The farmer and his wife do, too.
The chickens and ducks are frightened.
They run away.
But where are the rabbits?
They are eating Nicky's crackers.

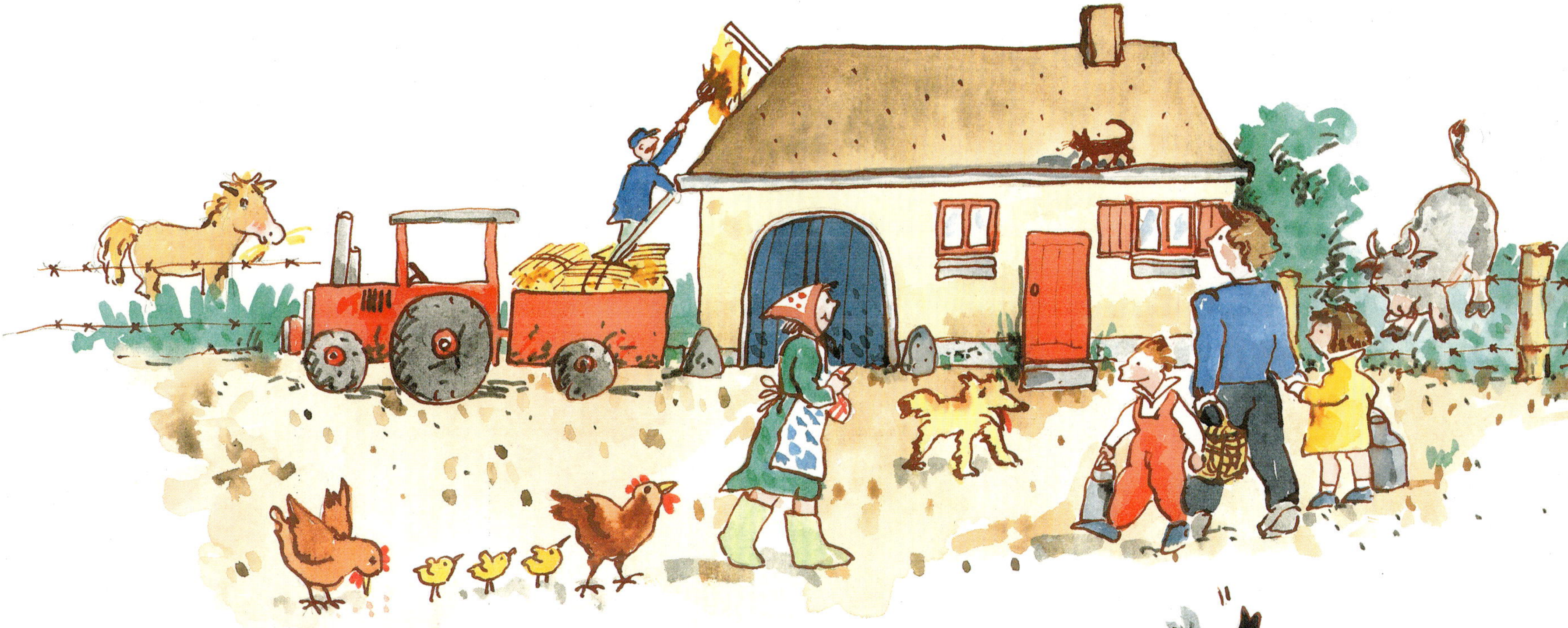

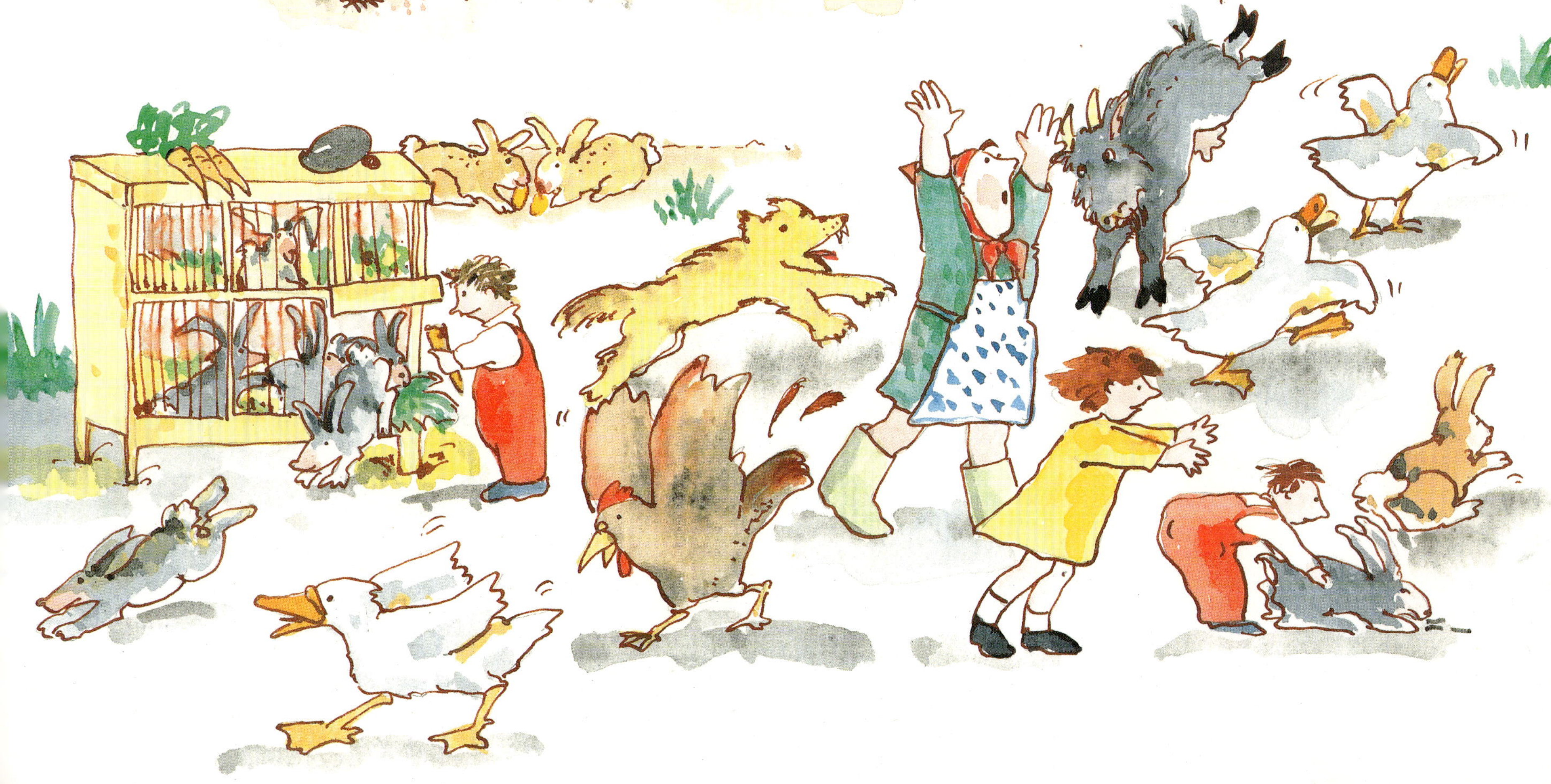

THE MOSQUITO

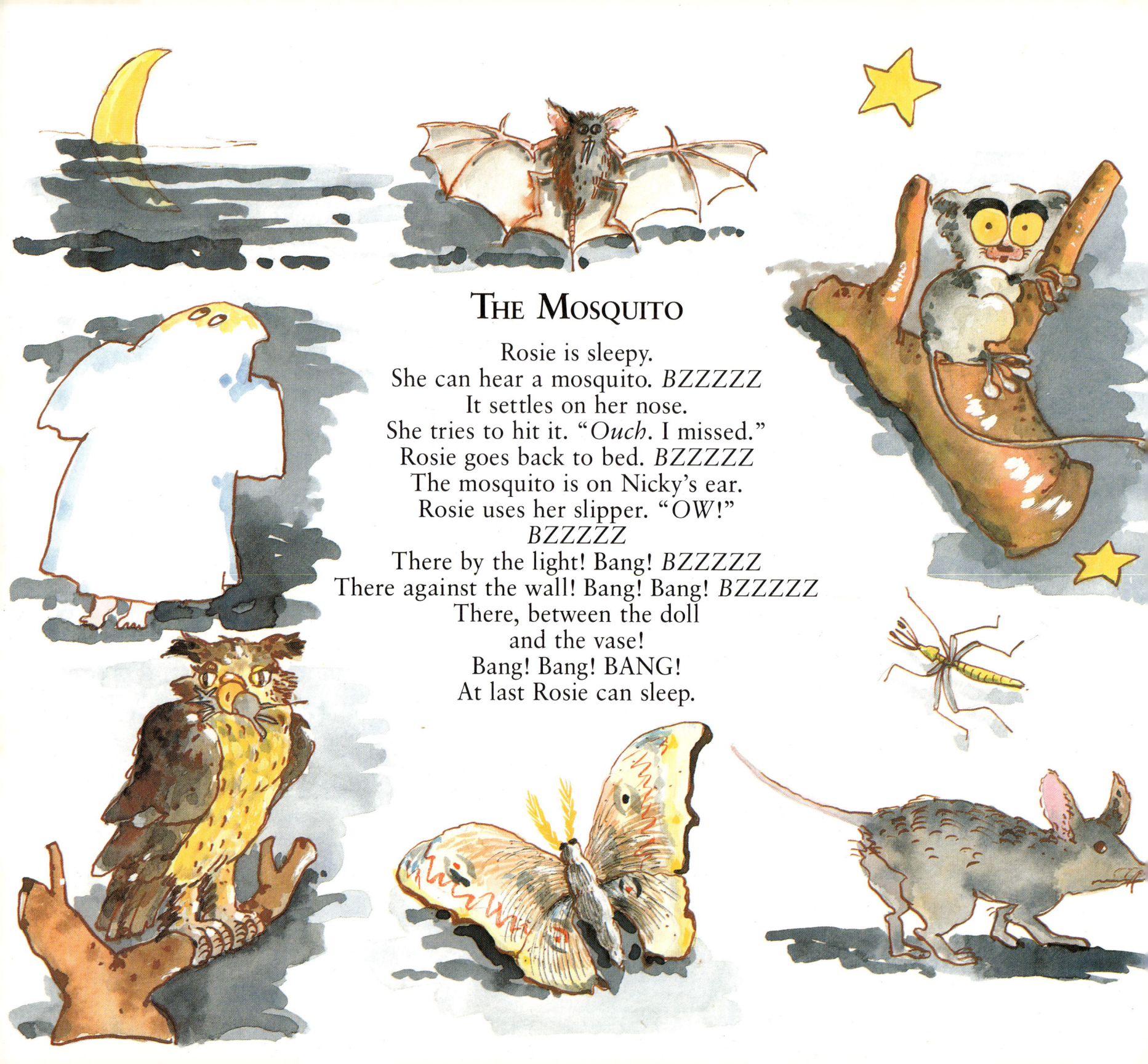

Rosie is sleepy.
She can hear a mosquito. *BZZZZZ*
It settles on her nose.
She tries to hit it. "*Ouch*. I missed."
Rosie goes back to bed. *BZZZZZ*
The mosquito is on Nicky's ear.
Rosie uses her slipper. "OW!"
BZZZZZ
There by the light! Bang! *BZZZZZ*
There against the wall! Bang! Bang! *BZZZZZ*
There, between the doll
and the vase!
Bang! Bang! BANG!
At last Rosie can sleep.

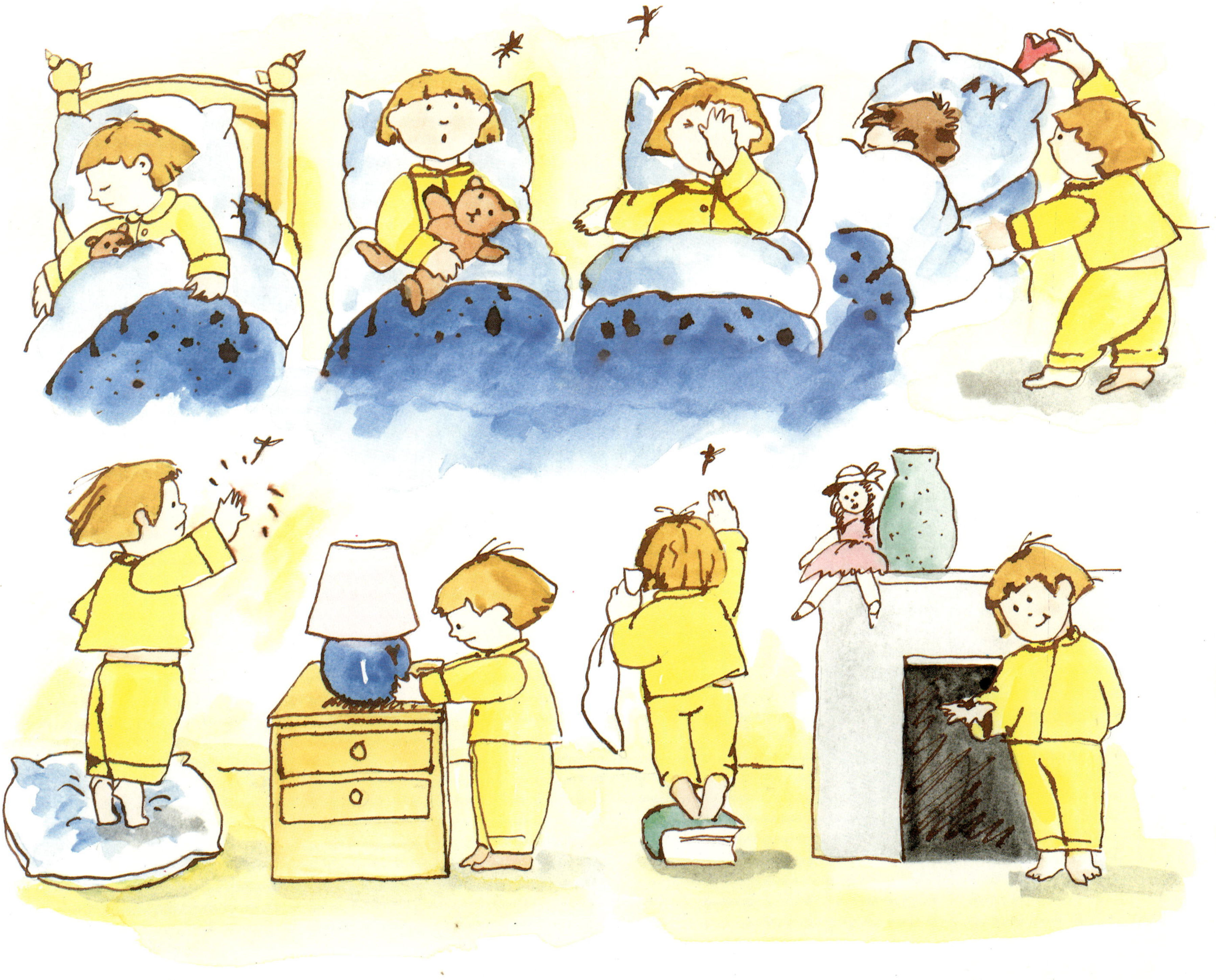